WILDFLOWERS

OF

GRAND TETON

AND

YELLOWSTONE

NATIONAL PARKS

including the Greater Yellowstone Ecosystem

Richard J. Shaw

Professor Emeritus and Emeritus Director
of Intermountain Herbarium, Department of Biology,
Utah State University, Logan, Utah

Wheelwright Press, Ltd.
1836 Sunnyside Avenue
Salt Lake City, Utah 84108

ACKNOWLEDGMENT

The publisher wishes to acknowledge the cooperative efforts of the Board and staff of Grand Teton Natural History Association and the Naturalist staff of Grand Teton National Park. The Association's generous financial contribution made possible the new photography. The Naturalist staff addressed the issue of wildflowers to be included, and reviewed the new manuscript. In particular, I would like to thank Grand Teton National Park Naturalists Linda Olson, Eddie Bowman, Don Cushman and Sharlene Milligan, Executive Director of the Grand Teton Natural History Association, for their efforts in reviewing and selecting photographs from the many submissions.

ISBN 0-937512-05-2

INTRODUCTION

The purpose of this book is to picture and describe the beautiful wildflowers of Yellowstone and Grand Teton National Parks as well as other areas included in the Greater Yellowstone Ecosystem. Besides the two parks, the system encompasses seven national forests, three national wildlife refuges, and one mountain range administered by the Bureau of Land Management, plus state and private lands. This huge complex sprawls across the northwest corner of Wyoming and large sections of Montana and Idaho. This book includes 102 common, herbaceous, flowering plants of the area which can be readily seen from the highway and nearby trails. While the majority of wildflowers are naturally occurring, a number of alien species have been included because they have become permanently established. We hope the brief descriptions and color photographs help you identify and enjoy the flowers you see and smell (but do not pick) in the Greater Yellowstone Ecosystem.

OBSERVING WILDFLOWERS

While wildlife observation will probably always take precedent over wildflower viewing, there is great satisfaction and a sense of accomplishment in being able to identify the flowers of this varied landscape. To understand the annual life cycles of these herbaceous plants and the ways in which they cope with changing environments around them is intriguing.

Look for specific things as you observe the plant in its natural setting. Does it grow in dense shade or full sunlight, gravelly or loam rich soil? Observe the blooming time and other plants that are growing in the same habitat. Particularly note the structure of the flower and try to determine the method by which it will be pollinated and the way in which its seeds will be dispersed. If you take notes of your observations, you can use them later in establishing your own wildflower garden or completing your data base for your wildflower photo collection. In any event, however, you will have learned something about the complexity and beauty of these biological advertising agents — the wildflowers.

Wildflowers are colorful, appealing miracles which we all occasionally discover. What many do not realize though, is the fact that flowers are not there for us; their beauty is not there for our pleasure. Biological function lies beneath the charming surface of the flower. In reality, survival is at stake. What strongly appeals to our human sensations are really finely tuned masterpieces of biological adaptations.

We cannot satisfactorily understand flowers unless we know something about the agents of pollination — insects, birds, mammals, wind and water. Flowers and animal pollinating agents are in a balanced trading agreement: food in exchange for pollination. It might be a shock to some, but the variable patterns of brilliant colors, many subtle fragrances and flower shapes have all evolved because it was advantageous to offer rewards and color beacons to insects and other animal visitors searching for nectar and pollen. It is a competitive world, and each species has survived by developing its own identifying characteristics to make it distinguishable from other plants in the same habitat. Another fact that has eluded us is that the fascinating spectrum of interactions between flowers and animal visitors that we see today is the result of millions of years of coevolution of plants and animals.

PLANT NAMES

In this book the common name which is the most popular in our area is mentioned first, but it should be understood that common names are not universally accepted and are not applied with any set of accepted rules. The result can often be confusion as each geographical area tends to concoct its own common names. Scientific names on the other hand are based on international rules which use a standardized two-part naming system called binomial nomenclature. The first part of a scientific name is the genus (genera for the plural form) and the second part of the name is the specific epithet. Thus every plant species has two names — the generic name and the specific epithet. This name will be accepted around the world and cannot be changed unless certain international rules of nomenclature are followed.

Scientific names have Latin endings and are usually italicized in print. Botanical scientific names are easier to pronounce than they may appear to be. Generally, you simply say the word as you would any English word. Regardless of how many syllables the word has, pronounce each syllable as you would in any ordinary word, slowly and distinctly. Don't worry about stressing any one syllable.

Examples:

Medicago sativa   MED-i-CAW-go sah-TIE-vah
Cynoglossum officinale   Sy-no-GLOSS-um Oh-fiss-in-AL-ee

PLANT ARRANGEMENT

To aid in rapid recognition, the photographs are arranged into five color groups: 1) green to cream-colored to white, 2) yellow to orange, 3) pink to red, 4) blue to purple, and 5) brown to reddish-brown. Such a scheme of identification has its limitations, especially in the pink to red and blue to purple categories. Because of individual color perceptions and environmental response, be sure to check another likely color if there is any question. Remember that some species will have intergrading specimens when it comes to petal color.

A WORD OF CAUTION

Picking wildflowers or collecting specimens of animals, trees, minerals or archeological artifacts in all National Parks and Monuments is prohibited without special permission from the park superintendent. Study the plants where they grow, take home photographs of them, but leave them for the enjoyment of those who will follow.

MARSH MARIGOLD
Caltha leptosepala

Buttercup Family

For the alpine hiker the excitement of this plant comes with the discovery that blue colored buds push through the melting snow, and within 48 hours these blue buds expand into beautiful white blossoms, 1 to 2 inches in diameter, similar to buttercups and anemones. The flowers of this genus lack petals, but the sepals are petaloid and showy. Each flower has many stamens and 5 or more pistils. The leaves are basal, succulent, and without lobes or divisions. Some authors have recommended this plant as an edible pot herb; however, it has been established that the leaves contain helleborin which has a burning taste and is also toxic. Two boilings with a change of water supposedly removes the poison. *Leptosepala* means "delicate" or "narrow," referring to the sepals.

WOODLAND STRAWBERRY
Rose Family
Fragaria vesca
This familiar wildflower and fruit inhabits the Lodgepole Pine and Aspen forests. Even though it lacks erect stems, it produces horizontal stolons or runners which, in turn, form new plants at their terminus. Such vegetative reproduction is very efficient. Each flower bears 5 green sepals, 5 rounded petals and numerous stamens. The pistils are numerous on a conical hump of tissue which becomes part of the edible fruit. Many of the wild strawberries have a more tart flavor than the cultivated varieties. A great variety of wildlife enjoy the berries. Herbalists of the 17th century had a high regard for the strawberry's medicinal properties.

ARCTIC GENTIAN
Gentian Family
Gentiana algida
Gentians are among our most esteemed wildflowers, being most abundant in the subalpine and alpine regions around the world. The calyx of the flower is a cup or a tube with 4 or 5 teeth; the corolla forms a tube or funnel with 4 or 5 lobes. Arctic Gentian is easily recognized by its greenish-white corolla which is spotted with dark purple. The basal and stem leaves are long and narrow with a smooth margin. Blossoming occurs in August and September, especially on Beartooth Pass. *Algida* means "cold," referring to the severe climate of the alpine ecosystem. The generic name, *Gentiana,* is named for Gentius, a king of Illyria who thought the plant had medicinal properties.

TUFTED EVENING PRIMROSE
Oenothera caespitosa

Evening Primrose Family

This plant is also known as Moonrose and is found on open sunny slopes. Little or no stem is visible above the ground, but flowers are composed of 4 sepals, 4 petals, 8 stamens and 4 stigmas. The sweet scented blossoms are 2 to 2½ inches broad. When the flowers first open, they are white but turn pink as they mature. Nectar glands are situated at the base of the hypanthium or floral tube, which may be as much as 3 inches long. Only those insects, such as Hawkmoths, with long mouthparts are capable of reaching the nectar. The ovary usually remains somewhat hidden among the leaves and matures into a many seeded capsule.

SMALLFLOWERED WOODLANDSTAR
Saxifrage Family
Lithophragma parviflorum

This small herbaceous species extends from the sagebrush community to meadows and open forests. Most of its leaves are at the base of the stem with a more or less lobed leaf blade. The flowers are in racemes with pink or white petals over ¼ inch long. Note how each petal is deeply cleft into 2 to 4 narrow lobes, a feature that suggests the common name. Within the calyx and corolla are 10 stamens. The generic name comes from the Greek words *lithos,* "stone," and *phragma,* "rock," apparently referring to the plant's habitat. The flowering stage occurs in June.

COMMON BEARGRASS
Xerophyllum tenax   Lily Family

While limited to the southern part of Yellowstone and the northern part of Grand Teton, this species is very striking when it covers an open slope with flowering stems up to 5 feet tall. The base of the plant has a mass of wiry grass-like leaves. The edges of the leaves are rough to the touch because of short stiff hairs. The flowers are borne in dense racemes which may be 6 to 8 inches long. The leaves arise from a thick rhizome, and any particular offshoot may not flower for several years. Ultimately an erect flowering stalk will arise and die down after fruiting. Like most lilies the individual small flowers are arranged on a plan of 3: 3 sepals, 3 petals and 6 stamens. Indian Basketgrass is another common name because Native Americans used the fibrous leaves to weave baskets. Elk and bighorn sheep eat the blossoms.

RICHARDSON GERANIUM   Geranium Family
Geranium richardsonii

Because of the long-beaked fruit many species of this genus are known by the name of Cranesbill. Like its relative, *G. viscosissimum,* Richardson Geranium begins to bloom in June and continues into August. However, its habitat requirement is quite different. Instead of the sagebrush community or open woods, the Richardson Geranium grows in moist Aspen woodland often by a small stream. Sometimes freezing temperatures in mid-June will break down the leaf chlorophyll producing a premature fall coloration. The five parts of the ovary separate and the seeds are catapulted outward by the curving segments of the style.

GREEN GENTIAN　　　　　　　　Gentian Family
Frasera speciosa

GREEN GENTIAN　　　　　　　　Gentian Family
Frasera speciosa

The showy Green Gentian, one of the tallest of the herbaceous plants, has a thick stem (up to 1½ inches in diameter) with a curious mixture of numerous leaves and greenish flower whorls. Each individual flower has a plan of 4 narrow sepals, 4 broad petals and 4 stamens. Many insects are attracted to the rather elaborate nectar glands and purple spots on each petal. While the plant is perennial, it flowers only once and then dies. It can be seen along the Jackson Hole Highway, Dunraven Pass, or even in the alpine zone of the Teton Range. The specific epithet, *speciosa*, means showy or beautiful and refers to the flowers.

9

SICKLETOP LOUSEWORT, PARROTS-BEAK
Figwort Family
Pedicularis racemosa

The white flowers and simple toothed leaves of the Parrots-beak distinguish it from the other common species of this genus. The curving and flattening of the 2 upper petals are responsible for the common name. The united upper petals enclose the anthers and taper into a slender downcurved beak almost touching the prominent lower lip. Flowering time varies from late June to August. The generic name, *Pedicularis*, is derived from the Latin meaning "louse" and relates to an ancient superstition that the use of the plants in this genus for livestock food caused louse infestation. This species can be found in coniferous forests or dry meadows in both parks.

COMMON COWPARSNIP
Heracleum lanatum   Carrot Family

This hairy perennial herb is 3 to 8 feet tall and features flower clusters 4 to 6 inches broad. It is found in moist meadows and stream sides in the valleys and up to mid-elevations in the canyons. The base of the leaves forms a conspicuous sheath around the coarse stem. The umbel is compound and consists of 15 to 30 umbellets; the outer flowers of each umbel have larger petals. The stems and leaves are eaten by a variety of large animals including elk and black bears. To render the stems palatable to humans, they can be peeled and boiled in two waters. However, no member of the Carrot Family should be eaten unless positive identification is possible.

AMERICAN BISTORT

Buckwheat Family

Polygonum bistortoides

A frequent herb of subalpine meadows and stream banks, American Bistort has a flowering stem 12 to 24 inches high. If viewed from a distance, the crowded cluster of flowers has the appearance of a tuft of wool or cotton. The individual flowers are small and bear 5 petaloid parts with exserted stamens. The rhizomes of this species have often been used by the Indians who prize them highly for their starchy and rather pleasant taste. The name, bistort, comes from the Latin words meaning "twice twisted," referring to the gnarled appearance of the dark brown rhizomes. Herbalists of the past recommended boiling the rhizomes in wine and using this decoction to treat diarrhea and dysentery.

HOT ROCK PENSTEMON

Figwort Family

Penstemon deustus

Most Penstemons have blue to lavender flowers in our area, but the species pictured is white to cream with conspicuous purple guide lines within the corolla tube (½ inch long). Note that the flower has bilateral symmetry with the upper lip consisting of 2 lobes and the lower lip with 3 lobes bent downward. The fifth stamen lacks an anther and is sterile. Most species in this large genus lack fragrant flowers, but this species has a mildly unpleasant odor. Look for this more or less woody plant in dry, open, often rocky sites from 6,000 to 8,500 feet.

LADIES-TRESSES; PEARL TWIST
Orchid Family
Spiranthes romanzoffiana

The creamy-white flowers of this plant are best appreciated with the aid of a hand lens. Like other orchid flowers, there are 3 sepals, 3 petals, and the stamens and pistil are combined into one unit. The small blossoms spiral up the slender 8 to 10 inch stem and appear in August and September. Within the inflorescence each flower arises from the axil of a leafy bract. Slender, lance-shaped leaves, 3 to 5 inches long, sheath the base of the stem. A few scattered plants are seen in the canyons, but most of them are found beside drying ponds at lower elevations. The name, Ladies-tresses, originated nearly two centuries ago, because the flower arrangement had a resemblance to braided hair.

MANYFLOWERED PHLOX
Phlox Family
Phlox multiflora

Driving the Parkway between Grand Teton and Yellowstone during June, one can see this low mat-forming perennial. Open wooded areas are best for the growth of this plant, but it approaches treeline on such mountains as Mt. Washburn. The flowers of this genus are described as salverform, which means that the corolla has a definite tube crowned by lobes which extend at right angles. The stamens and style are contained within the tube. Only long-tongued insects such as butterflies and moths have access to the nectar at the base of the tube. This phlox species often grows with Moss Campion and Alpine Forget-me-not and follows dry mountain ridges in the alpine zone.

CANADA VIOLET
Viola canadensis   Violet Family

This rather tall perennial violet has a wide distribution within North America. Recognition is relatively easy because of the white flowers and leaf blades which are often wider than long and broadly heart-shaped. Even though the petals appear snow white, the throat of the flower changes abruptly to lemon yellow. The lower petal of this bilaterally symmetrical flower has several distinctive purple lines that are called guide lines by students of pollination. There is good evidence that these lines direct insect visitors past the stamens to the sweet nectar in the basal spur. Harrington suggests that all species of violets are edible either raw in salads or cooked as pot herbs. Usually this species is found in moist montane forests where it flowers in late June and early July.

FRINGED GRASS-OF-PARNASSUS
Parnassia fimbriata Saxifrage Family

Around the lakes and along the streams of the canyons in late July and August this white-flowered *Parnassia* will surely catch your eye. The solitary flowers are on the ends of stems 3 to 12 inches high. The photograph highlights the daintily fringed petals which are so characteristic of this species. Note also that there are 5 white fertile stamens alternating with 5 yellow sterile stamens. The leaves are kidney or heart-shaped and have a smooth edge. The generic name refers to the mountain in Greece where the Muses of mythology lived.

COLORADO COLUMBINE

Buttercup Family

Aquilegia coerulea

Few wild flowers have the delicate or ornamental grace of this member of the Buttercup Family. Throughout July and August it brightens the canyon trails up to 9,500 feet. The plant has one or more stems 4 to 16 inches tall, and mostly basal leaves that are 3 parted and lobed. The flowers have 5 petals which are extended backward into conspicuous, long, hollow spurs. The sepals vary in color from blue to white. The numerous yellow stamens and 5 long pistils project beyond the flower face. *Aquilegia* comes from the Latin word *aquila* meaning "eagle," referring to the spurred petals which look like eagle talons. This columbine is the state flower of Colorado, and as one goes northward from Colorado, the blue color of the sepals fades to white or cream.

SEGO LILY

Lily Family

Calochortus nuttallii

The genus *Calochortus* is one of the most beautiful in the Lily Family, and is recognized by the narrow sepals in contrast to the broad conspicuously marked petals. The base of each petal has a round, yellow gland surrounded by bright yellow hairs and a purple crescent marking outward from the gland. The flowers rise several inches above the narrow, grass-like, basal leaves. Boiled bulbs have a flavor of potatoes and were eaten by the Indians and early western settlers when food was scarce. Several *Calochortus* species once thrived in many western states, but cities and towns encroaching upon the habitat have left some species in a precarious position. June and July are the months for blossoms.

WHITE DRYAS; MOUNTAIN DRYAD

Dryas octopetala   Rose Family

Growing in limestone rocks and windy exposed sites above treeline, this prostrate plant quickly catches one's eye because the flowers are so large (1½ inches in diameter) and the tufted fruits are so attractive. Many adaptations to severe climatic conditions are visible. For example, it has evergreen, leathery leaves with recurved margins to reduce water loss. It frequently grows with Arctic Willow. The 8 petals are responsible for the name, *octopetala,* and from the name, *Dryas,* comes the Greek word meaning "wood nymph." This is a circumboreal plant, occurring in the same habitat around the world in both arctic and alpine situations.

YAMPAH   Carrot Family

Perideridia montana

The individual flowers of this perennial herb are constructed on a plan of 5, clustered in compound umbels, a feature common to all members of this family. This is an erect and slender plant that grows from 1 to 3 feet tall. As an important food plant of the Indians and mountain men, it was recognized by its slender leaves and its 2 to 3 fleshy roots just below the ground level. When eaten raw, these roots have a sweet, nutty, parsnip-like flavor. They can also be boiled, roasted or dried. When thinking about eating any member of the Carrot Family, positive identification is essential. Some species are the most violently poisonous plants in the North Temperate Zone.

ENGELMANN ASTER   Sunflower Family
Aster engelmannii
Making the distinction between members of the genus, *Aster,* and the genus, *Erigeron,* (Daisies), is not easy. Many technical features are needed for identification. However, this species is easily recognized by such reliable criteria as disk flowers surrounded by 15 to 19 white ray flowers that may be 1 inch long. The leaves are lanceolate or elliptic and nearly smooth. The slightly hairy stem may reach a height of 3 feet. The greenish bracts, which enclose the flowers in bud, form a structure known as an involucre; and, therefore, each bract is called an involucral bract. The leaves may be boiled as greens. This attractive plant can be found at 9,000 feet on Mt. Washburn or in the shade around Jenny Lake in late summer.

COMMON YARROW   Sunflower Family
Achillea millefolium
Before this aromatic perennial produces flowers, it is sometimes mistaken for a fern because of its much divided leaves. This pinnate dissection of the leaves is tied to the specific epithet, *millefolium,* meaning a "thousand leaflets." The composite flowering head has both ray and disk flowers, and the corolla color is mostly white and occasionally pink. This plant is known throughout the northern hemisphere from sea level to the alpine zone. With such genetic plasticity it is easy to see why several subspecies have been proposed. The generic name, *Achillea,* is named for Achilles, who is supposed to have used yarrow to heal his wounded warriors after the siege of Troy.

WHITE MULES EAR; WHITEHEAD WYETHIA
Sunflower Family
Wyethia helianthoides

In open wet meadows north of Colter Bay and especially on Fountain Flats in Yellowstone one can find this most striking white flowered composite. The broad lanceolate leaves are traceable to the common name, and the generic name is in honor of N. J. Wyeth, an explorer of the West in the 1830's. The plant stands 2 feet tall and blends well with the Blue Camas of wet meadows. The leafy hairy stems grow from a cluster of basal leaves and have a composite head with about 13 to 15 white or pale cream ray flowers. The numerous disk flowers are yellow. The young plants are eaten by elk and deer. Flowering occurs in June.

WILD BUCKWHEAT
Buckwheat Family
Eriogonum umbellatum

Also known as Sulphur Flower, this plant is especially showy from sagebrush flat to mountain ridges. The sulphur-yellow blossoms are in umbrella-like clusters at the top of a 10 to 12 inch flowering stalk, while the numerous leaves grow near the ground and accumulate bits of organic matter to enrich the soil. Each individual flower has 6 perianth parts which cannot be separated into sepals or petals. A related species, *E. ovalifolium,* is widely distributed and extends upwards even above treeline where it becomes dwarfed and cushion-like. The best recognition feature of *E. ovalifolium,* is lack of any leaves or bracts on the stem. The genus *Eriogonum* is taxonomically difficult and has at least 250 species, mostly in western United States.

FENDLER MEADOWRUE
Thalictrum fendleri Buttercup Family

Mountain meadows and moist open forests are the habitat of Fendler Meadowrue. The common name comes from its resemblance to Common Rue *(Ruta)* which is grown for its medicinal properties. Meadowrue's fernlike foliage is often confused with the related columbines. The branched, sometimes purplish stems can reach a height of 2 feet. This species is dioecious, meaning that one plant bears only male flowers and another different plant will bear only female flowers. These unisexual flowers are unique in that they have 5 inconspicuous green sepals, but no petals.

The downward hanging, male flowers are most apt to catch one's eye because the numerous, greenish anthers dangle from fragile filaments and the whole flower has the appearance of a lamp shade with a fringe on the bottom. The female flowers bear 6 to 10 pistils. Flowering occurs in June and July.

DOUGLAS CHAENACTIS
Chaenactis douglasii

Sunflower Family

This plant has inspired a number of common names including: False Yarrow, Pincushion Plant, Brides Bouquet, Dusty Maiden, and Hoary Chaenactis. Such names reflect features of the composite head and foliage. Ray flowers are lacking, and only white to pink tubular disk flowers are present in the ½ inch head. A basal rosette of leaves appears first, and these are followed by a leafy stem 12 to 20 inches tall. The individual leaves are fernlike because they are mostly pinnately dissected. Dry, gravelly, road side cuts are the best sites to watch for this species during July and August. An alpine species, *C. alpina,* has a more pink disk flower and a small stature of about 3 inches.

WESTERN VALERIAN
Valerian Family
Valeriana occidentalis

Valerians in general tend to be strongly aromatic. The roots, particularly, have a foul odor. This valerian is a robust plant 1 to 3 feet tall with long stalked, broad-bladed, basal leaves. The opposite leaves may have side segments nearly ½ inch wide, and an end lobe up to 4 inches in length. The calyx is initially inconspicuous, but later unrolls and enlarges to crown the fruit with numerous feathery bristles by which it becomes readily airborne. The corolla consists of 5 petals fused into a tube. Three stamens and a one-seeded ovary complete the delicate flower. Extracts of roots and rhizomes have been used as a sedative for "nervous disorders." This species inhabits moist ground from foothills to subalpine.

ALPINE SUNFLOWER; RYDBERGIA   Sunflower Family
Hymenoxys grandiflora

The almost perfect symmertry of the ray and disk flowers of this alpine species are in sharp contrast to the rocky, limestone slopes and ridges where it is found. The flowering head is 2 to 3 inches in diameter, and each ray flower has 3 lobes at the tip. Another common name, Old-Man-of-the-Mountain, refers to the dense hairs on the stems and leaves. This pubescence reduces water loss, traps heat, and protects against strong ultra-violet radiation. The flowering heads usually face east perhaps as a protection from the prevailing wind. Zwinger and Willard (see references) state that each plant stores food over several years until it has sufficient nutrients and energy to blossom, and after the fruits and seeds mature the entire plant dies.

HAIRY GOLDEN ASTER
Heterotheca villosa
Sunflower Family

Species of this genus resemble the genus *Aster* in a number of ways, but differ in that the ray flowers are yellow instead of being white to purple. One feature, visible with a hand lens, is the presence of 2 whorls of pappus, the outer whorl being shorter than the inner whorl. Stems of the species illustrated grow 6 to 20 inches tall, bloom mostly in August and are common around the buildings at Old Faithful. *Villosa* means "hairy," referring to the soft pubescence which covers the stem and leaves. This covering is not sticky as it is in the Gumweed. This is a very complex and confusing species consisting of several varieties differing in pubescence and other details.

MULES-EAR WYETHIA
Wyethia amplexicaulis
Sunflower Family

The shiny, green leaves of this plant are 8 to 20 inches long and, in general, have the shape of a mule's ear; hence the common name. The specific epithet, *amplexicaulis*, is from the Latin *amplex* meaning "embrace" and *caulis* meaning "stem" and refers to the way that the leaves clasp the stem. While the bright yellow, 2 to 4 inch heads are similar to the Balsamroots, it can be easily distinguished. The Balsamroots' leaves are arrowhead-shaped or divided, often pubescent, and arise from the base of the stem. The generic name, *Wyethia*, is in honor of Capt. N. J. Wyeth who crossed the continent with an early botanist in 1834. Late June brings forth the flowers.

21

NODDING BEGGARTICKS; BUR-MARIGOLD
Sunflower Family

Bidens cernua

At the edge of ponds this freely branching herb will bloom in late July and August. The opposite leaves are sharply toothed and may unite around the stem. The flowering heads are usually 1½ inches across. The fruits, called achenes, are equipped with downward pointing spines which catch on the fur of passing animals thus aiding in dispersing the species. Two distinct rows of green bracts are directly below the golden ray flowers. Some species of Beggarticks lack the ray flowers and are considered as unattractive weeds. The generic name, *Bidens,* means "two teeth," referring to the pappus.

ONE-FLOWER HELIANTHELLA
Sunflower Family

Helianthella uniflora

This species of *Helianthella* and its close relative, *H. quinquenervis,* can be easily confused with the Common Sunflower *(Helianthus annuus)* and possibly the Showy Goldeneye *(Viguiera multiflora).* The leaves of *Helianthella* lack teeth, and the flowering heads are borne singly, being 1½ to 2½ inches in diameter. To separate the species illustrated here from *H. quinquenervis* check the back side of the leaves for prominent veins. *H. uniflora* has 3 and *H. quinquenervis* has 5. Look for the Helianthellas in moist soil and open woods during July and August.

GOATSBEARD;
YELLOW SALSIFY
Sunflower Family
Tragopogon dubius

This old-world species is an invader of waste places and roadside cuts. Its rapid spread in this country is due in part to the light dandelion-like fruits which are carried great distances by the wind. The delicate fibers at the top of each achene act much like a parachute. The plant is also known as Noonflower because the flowering heads are open only in the morning. All species of *Tragopogon* have edible, nutritious taproots which to some people taste like parsnips. When the stems or leaves are cut a milky juice is exuded. Although Goatsbeard was once favored for the treatment of heartburn and kidney stones, such use is no longer recommended.

BALSAMROOT
Sunflower Family
Balsamorhiza sagittata

The June visitor frequently confuses this common plant with a series of sunflower-like species, but careful examination reveals many striking differences. The numerous basal leaves are arrowhead-shaped and covered with tiny, silvery hairs. The stems are 1 to 2 feet tall, bearing solitary heads at their apex. The deep, penetrating roots and ripe achenes of this plant were used by Native Americans as a source of natural food. Balsamroots are inhabitants of sagebrush flats and dry, rocky ridges in open forests. Where two or more species of *Balsamorhiza* grow together they may form intermediate hybrids.

COMMON RABBITBRUSH   Sunflower Family
Chrysothamnus nauseosus

Rabbitbrush plants inhabit the semiarid areas of both parks and their adjacent boundary lands. During most of the summer, these plants are unattractive, but in late August and early September the bushes become covered with numerous heads of golden-yellow flowers. Many insect pollinators are attracted to these masses of flowers even though the individual heads lack the ray flowers so common to other members of the family. Besides furnishing useful cover in open areas, Common Rabbitbrush is important to wildlife as the foliage and seeds are readily consumed, especially by rabbits and hoofed browsers. This species is 2 to 3 feet tall, and both stems and leaves are covered with a dense woolly mat of whitish hairs.

HEARTLEAF ARNICA
Arnica cordifolia   Sunflower Family

This aromatic perennial inhabits coniferous forests throughout the Rocky
Mountain region and has received its
common name from the fact that
basal leaves and leaves of stems are
markedly heart-shaped at the base.
The plants are mostly 7 to 13 inches
tall and the flowering heads are 2 to
3 inches in diameter. Blossoming begins in mid-June and lasts until mid-
July. A few individuals start to
bloom again in early September. The
leaves have a sawtooth margin and
the plant spreads from extensive
rhizomes. Various species of *Arnica*
have been used medicinally in
Europe since the 16th century, but
our species has been listed in the
Southwest as a poisonous plant because of the presence of arnicin, a
crystalline toxin, found in the leaves.

CANADA GOLDENROD
Sunflower Family
Solidago canadensis

It is difficult to separate the many
species of goldenrods found in North
America because the genus seems to
lack consistent distinguishing charac-
ters. The species in our parks are all
erect perennials, bearing alternate
leaves and small composite heads
containing both ray and disk flowers.
The many, small flowering heads are
arranged on only one side of the
spreading branches. The flowering
period is in August and September,
and this species grows in a variety of
dry, open sites. A persistent belief
that goldenrods are hay-fever plants
has been discredited by studies that
show the flowers are pollinated by
insects and that the pollen is relatively heavy, and therefore, poorly dispersed by the wind.

SHOWY GOLDENEYE   Sunflower Family
Viguiera multiflora
Long after the spring and summer flowers have faded from the mountain landscape, many roadsides are brightened by the golden-yellow heads of the Showy Goldeneye. This herb grows up to 3 feet tall, with few to several heads per stem. The leaves are lance-shaped and oppositely arranged at least in the lowermost part. The bright yellow ray flowers are ½ to 1 inch long. The disk flowers are accompanied by the scales called chaff, which partially envelop the achenes. The numerous disk flowers are also somewhat darker, suggesting a golden eye. There is growing evidence that this species is responsible for poisoning of grazing animals in the southwestern states.

YELLOW MONKEY-FLOWER
Mimulus guttatus   Figwort Family

Maturing in wet meadows and along stream banks, the Yellow Monkey-flower's bright yellow spotted petals draw immediate attention. Delicate hairs cover the three lower lobes of the corolla and, together with the orange spots, help to attract insect pollinators. Close examination of the stigma reveals 2 roundish lobes which are spread apart. When one of these lobes makes contact with a pollen-laden bee, the 2 stigma lobes immediately begin to come together like the leaves of a book. The pollen will thus be held firmly, and when the bee backs out of the corolla tube, no self-pollination will occur. The square stems have opposite leaves and are quite fragile because of their hollow structure. Height of the plant can vary from 4 to 20 inches.

LANCELEAVED STONECROP
Stonecrop Family
Sedum lanceolatum

Because of the succulent nature of their stems and leaves, the recognition of the genus *Sedum* is easy, but the separation of the species is confusing, calling for special attention to minute details. This plant has numerous basal leaves. While the leaves of the stem vary greatly in shape, they are not ridged underneath. Each flower, resembling a bright yellow star, has 5 petals, 8 to 10 stamens and 5 pistils which form 5 follicles when mature. Look for this species on rocks and gravelly soil, extending from the sagebrush flats upward into the alpine. Flowering occurs from late June through August, depending on elevation.

MOUNTAIN GOLDENPEA
Thermopsis rhombifolia   Pea Family

Because of a superficial resemblance this plant is frequently called False Lupine, but several distinctive features set it apart. The leaves are trifoliately compound with leaflets up to 3 inches long. The 10 stamens are always separate and distinct. As the petals fall off, the ovary elongates into a flat pea-like pod. Goldenpea is unpalatable to wildlife and grazing livestock so it may replace more desirable forage plants. There are reports that this legume contains a number of toxic alkaloids, especially in the seeds. This species can tolerate different habitats, including wet meadows, well drained soils and dry forest sites.

27

BUTTER-AND-EGGS; COMMON TOADFLAX
Linaria vulgaris   Figwort Family

Throughout North America the Butter-and-Eggs plant has become a familiar inhabitant of roadsides and disturbed sites. It closely resembles the cultivated snapdragon except that the inch-long corolla is spurred at the base. Slender stems, 1 to 2 feet tall and bearing numerous, narrowly linear leaves, arise from perennial roots. A native of Europe, this plant was a weed in the flax fields. In North America the species has often escaped cultivation and formed large patches from creeping rhizomes. Several other names, such as Bread-and-Cheese and Chopped-Eggs, refer to the orange and yellow corollas. The name, Toadflax, refers to the corolla's "mouth" resembling that of a toad, and the leaves which look like Flax leaves.

GLACIER LILY
Lily Family
Erythronium grandiflorum

Common names of plants frequently cause confusion among flower lovers because they vary so much in different geographical areas. For example, this plant is also known as Dogtooth Violet, Adders Tongue, Fawn Lily, and Trout Lily. In both parks the plants are often abundant above 7,500 feet. The yellow, nodding flowers are on a stem 6 to 12 inches high, and this stem arises from a bulb several inches below the soil surface. In this area almost all the flowers have yellow anthers but a few have red anthers. The 3 stigmas are diverging and slightly longer than the anthers. Flowering is from June to July depending on how rapidly the snow fields melt. Grizzly and black bears gather and eat the bulbs.

BLAZING STAR MENTZELIA

Blazing Star Family

Mentzelia laevicaulis

One reason that this plant draws such frequent comments is that it occupies unlikely sites, such as gravelly roadside cuts and dry streambeds where many plants fail to invade. The light yellow flowers which are 1 to 3 inches in diameter are borne in a branching inflorescence at the ends of 2 to 3 foot stems. The numerous stamens are nearly as long as the petals and fan outward in all directions. Because barb-like hairs on the leaves and stems adhere to clothing and to the hairs of animals, these plants are sometimes called Stikleleaf. Flowering begins in July and continues into September.

COMMON ST. JOHNWORT

St. Johnwort Family

Hypericum perforatum

This old-world species is a well established perennial weed over much of eastern and western United States. In the western states since 1900 it has acquired the name, Klamath-weed, and has become a serious pest in pastures and rangeland. It has spread in the two parks since 1971 and will undoubtedly invade any new disturbance sites that man creates. It is much taller than the native species, *H. formosum,* reaching up to 3 feet high. Even though this plant is poisonous to livestock, it has been used medicinally by the Native Americans and Europeans for many conditions from skin irritations to tuberculosis.

WESTERN WALLFLOWER
Erysimum asperum   Mustard Family

Within both parks there are many species of wild mustards, but this is the only one with flowers of any size over ½ inch. It is infrequent in dry stony places and the bright yellow petals are at least ½ inch long. The flowers also have 4 sepals, 6 stamens and distinctive elongated pod-like fruit, reaching a length of 2 to 3 inches. The 1 to 2 foot stems bear leaves which are narrow and sometimes have small teeth. The Zuni Indians ground this plant, mixed it with water, and applied it to their skin to prevent sunburn. The common name comes from related species that grew on ancient rock walls of Europe.

SUBALPINE BUTTERCUP   Buttercup Family
Ranunculus eschscholtzii

The waxy five-petaled flowers of this talus slope perennial typify the 12 or more buttercup species growing in the two parks. The plant has one to several stems, usually with yellow or brownish hairs below the flowers. There are 3 varieties of this species and these are separated on the variation of the basal leaves. They vary from shallowly 3-lobed to many divided segments. The numerous species of *Ranunculus* offer considerable difficulty in identification since some of the taxa will hybridize, leading to intermediate forms. Most buttercups grow in mesic to aquatic environments such as meadows, marshes, ponds or streams.

NUTTALL VIOLET
Violet Family
Viola nuttallii
There are at least two species of yellow violets which bloom during the first two weeks of June. The one pictured is the larger of the two and has the larger leaf. All violets have irregular flowers, consisting of 5 sepals, 5 petals and 5 stamens. The lowest petal bears a sac-like spur at its base and contains nectar. The whole flower arrangement, including the brownish to purple guide lines, favors cross pollination. The genus *Viola* is considered a critical group with many difficult species, primarily because they hybridize freely under natural conditions and in some cases they produce inconspicuous flowers and seeds hidden at the base of the plant.

YELLOW PONDLILY; SPATTERDOCK
Waterlily Family
Nuphar polysepalum
This large attractive aquatic plant grows from submerged rhizomes and bears long petioled leaves usually floating on the surfaces of beaver ponds and small lakes. The showy flowers are from 2 to 3 inches in diameter, having 5 to 6 sepals and many scale-like petals. The stamens are also numerous and close to the flattened stigma. The shiny green leaves are 6 to 15 inches long and 6 to 10 inches broad. The rhizomes are buried in the mud and were often eaten by the Native Americans. The Montana Indians parched the seeds or ground them into flour.

BRACTED LOUSEWORT; WOOD BETONY
Figwort Family
Pedicularis bracteosa

This perennial produces a stem up to 36 inches high and grows in moist, forested areas. The leaves are alternate, but the fern-like segments of each leaf are opposite. The flowers are in a terminal spike. Individual flowers are ½ to ¾ inch long and have a corolla with 2 lips, the upper lip longer and somewhat hood-like. The stigma protrudes beyond the upper lip. Elk are reported to eat the flowers and stems at the time of flowering in late June and July. Pollination in this genus is complex, usually requiring a specific bee pollinator.

YELLOWBELL; YELLOW FRITILLARY
Fritillaria pudica   Lily Family

Depending on elevation, the flowering stems appear in late May or early June in sagebrush habitats. The yellow or orange drooping flowers turn reddish as they age. The perianth parts are about ¾ of an inch long and, when they fall and the fruit starts to ripen, the stem straightens out, placing the 3-sectioned fruit in an erect position. The underground bulbs are 2 to 6 inches beneath the surface and reproduce asexually by forming tiny bulblets the size of corn kernels. While the bulbs and bulblets are edible, either raw or cooked, such use in National Parks and Monuments is not allowed.

OREGON GRAPE; CREEPING BARBERRY

Barberry Family

Mahonia repens

This perennial is so low that its woody nature is not evident. Every spring dense clusters of yellow flowers brighten the appearance of prickly evergreen leaves. Usually each flower has 6 sepals, 6 petals and 6 stamens. By August the plants have produced rather sparse clusters of grape-like fruit. Some people claim the berries have a bitter taste, but a number of authors recommend using them in making jelly, jam or wine. Along with the ripening of fruits, some of the pinnately compound leaves turn beautiful shades of red or purple. This species is most frequently found on well drained, morainal soil.

ORANGE AGOSERIS; MOUNTAIN DANDELION

Sunflower Family

Agoseris aurantiaca

Sometimes called False Dandelion, this plant is found in grassy meadows in open, coniferous forests. The solitary composite head is located on a leafless erect stem up to 20 inches high. When broken or cut, the stems and basal leaves exude a milky juice. All the flowers in the head are ray flowers. The fruits which follow have soft, white hairs which aid in dispersal. The specific epithet, *aurantiaca,* is derived from the Latin meaning "orange." However, the flowers may turn red-purple or pink with age. *Agoseris* leaves are narrow, stalkless and form a basal rosette. Flowering will continue from June through August.

FAIRYSLIPPER; CALYPSO ORCHID   Orchid Family
Calypso bulbosa

The Greater Yellowstone Ecosystem has at least 15 species of orchids, but this is the most beautiful and striking. It grows in deep shaded areas of the coniferous forests and blooms early in the summer season. Usually it has only one small green basal leaf which, along with stem, arises from a bulbous corm embedded frequently in decaying wood or organic matter. The flower resembles a small lady's slipper with its cup-like lip. Luer (see references) says the flowers are odorless and have no nectar. Pollination seems to be accomplished by means of insects that are visually deceived.

SPRINGBEAUTY
Purslane Family
Claytonia lanceolata
Springbeauties are widespread throughout both parks and are among the first flowers to follow retreating snowbanks. Usually several stems grow from a tuberous underground corm (stem). Each of these stems has 2 succulent leaves. Flower color varies from white to pink, and, in the whiter forms, pinkish veins add emphasis to the notched petals. There are 5 stamens and 2 sepals which remain long after the petals fall. The tuberous corms (½ to ¾ inch in diameter) were dug by Native Americans and eaten as we would eat potatoes. These plants are frequent from the valleys to the alpine in the Rocky Mountains.

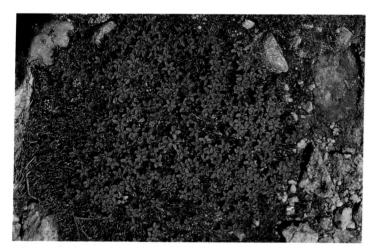

MOSS CAMPION
Pink Family
Silene acaulis
The small branches of this perennial plant form a tightly interwoven cushion connecting to a deep penetrating taproot. In the alpine ecosystem such a growth habit raises the temperature inside the cushion and helps to create a microclimate which is more suitable for survival. Zwinger and Willard (see references) report that a Moss Campion plant may be ten years old before flowering begins since early growth energy goes into establishing a root system up to four to five feet deep that accumulates water and anchors the plant against almost constant wind. Each pink flower has 5 notched petals, 5 sepals and 10 delicate stamens. The leaves are short, narrow and very close together, giving the cushion a mosslike appearance. In both parks this species inhabits rocky exposed sites over 9,800 feet.

STICKY GERANIUM
Geranium Family
Geranium viscosissimum

This beautiful herbaceous species is found in sagebrush, grasslands and open woods. It has strong branching stems from 15 to 30 inches tall and deeply-lobed leaves. The rose-lavender flowers (1 to 1½ inches in diameter) are constructed on a plan of five; i.e., all parts are five or multiples of five. The capsule-like fruit, typical of the family, is beaked due to the elongation of the style. As the capsule ripens, its longitudinal sections open with such recoiling force that the seeds are catapulted outward from the parent plant several feet. Leaves of the stem and some flower parts are covered with sticky glandular hairs. Flowering occurs from June through late August.

TWINFLOWER
Honeysuckle Family
Linnaea borealis

The Swedish botanist, Linnaeus, who established our binomial system of nomenclature, had a favorite flower, the Twinflower, and in 1737 this plant was named to honor him. This creeping, evergreen herb is found in open to dense, moist coniferous forests and has a circumboreal distribution. From the trailing branches rise flower stalks which bear 2 pendant pink flowers. The corolla is almost equally 5-lobed, but there are only 4 stamens. Its tiny dry fruits are sticky because of hooked bristles which become readily attached to animals and birds. Its blossoms appear in July and August.

PRINCE'S PINE; PIPSISSEWA
Wintergreen Family
Chimaphila umbellata

This plant is a trailing and somewhat woody perennial with leafy shoots and flowering branches. In both parks it is found in the shade of coniferous trees which surround the lakes. The narrowly wedge-shaped leaves are evergreen and have margins with forward pointing teeth. The flowers, borne in small umbellate clusters, are pink and contain 10 distinctive stamens radiating around an unusually stout green ovary. If a hand lens is used to look at the stamens, the purple anthers reveal terminal pores through which pollen is shed much like salt grains come out of a salt shaker. The name, Pipsissewa, is evidently of Native American origin, and the plant was used for a variety of ailments such as rheumatism and fevers. The flowers appear in late July or early August.

PARRY PRIMROSE   Primrose Family
Primula parryi
One of the largest alpine herbaceous plants stands out conspicuously along streams and below melting snowbanks because of the magenta flowers. Several flowers, each on a nodding pedicel, are clustered at the top of a leafless stem. Close examination of a flower reveals that the 5 petal lobes are joined at their base into a narrow tube. These flowers have the odor of carrion and undoubtedly attract flies to accomplish pollination. Leaves are basal and somewhat succulent. The specific epithet honors C. C. Parry, an 1800's botanist who collected many plants in the Western States. July and August are the best months for flowering.

CANADA THISTLE   Sunflower Family
Cirsium arvense
This Eurasian invader is now a cosmopolitan weed mainly because it not only produces parachute-like fruits, but it also forms creeping rhizomes that produce dense continuous populations. The plants are 2 to 5 feet high and bear numerous small flowering heads. The pinkish-purple flowers add a decorative touch to some roadside cuts. This creeping thistle is unique among thistles of our area in that there are male and female flower heads, and these are on separate plants. The flower heads are filled with nectar and attract a variety of pollinating agents. Young leaves, tender roots and flower heads may be used for food in times of emergency.

PRAIRIESMOKE

Geum triflorum   Rose Family

The nodding flowers and heads of feathery styles have been responsible for many common names, such as Old Mans Whiskers, China Bells and Long-plummed Avens. The stems are 7 to 18 inches high and have mostly basal and fern-like leaves. The whole plant is softly hairy, and this feature makes it challenging as a photographic subject. After fertilization the bell-shaped flowers turn upward and the numerous styles elongate so that the wind will eventually disperse the seeds. The Blackfeet Indians are reported to have used the root of this plant as an eye wash. Look for the flowers in June and early July in open meadows, hillsides and ridges.

PINK WINTERGREEN; SHINLEAF
Pyrola asarifolia   Wintergreen Family

The nodding flowers are light pink to rosy-red and are arranged in slender racemes on stems 8 to 15 inches high. There are 5 petals and 10 stamens, the anthers of which release their pollen through terminal pores. The style is characteristically bent to one side and often has a ring or collar below the stigma. The kidney shaped leaves are basal, relatively thick and shiny. Look for this evergreen perennial in wet soil around streams and in the shade of coniferous forests. The fruit is a dry capsule. There are at least 4 other related species of *Pyrola* in the Greater Yellowstone Ecosystem

GLOBEMALLOW; WILD HOLLYHOCK
Iliamna rivularis   Mallow Family

Along streams and roadsides from Mammoth Hot Springs south to Teton Pass the gorgeous pink flowers of Globemallow add their distinctive color during July and August. The stems are stout, branched and reach a height of 4 or 5 feet. The maple-like leaves are 2 to 8 inches across, generally with 5 lobes. The individual flowers are up to 2 inches broad and resemble cultivated hollyhocks. Irritating hairs cover the fruits which break open like segments of oranges. In some areas of the Rocky Mountains this is one of the first herbaceous species to appear after a forest fire. The seeds require some heat from fires or scouring to germinate.

LONGLEAF PHLOX   Phlox Family
Phlox longifolia
The leaves of many western species of Phlox are short and needle-like, but this species has narrow, linear blades up to an inch long. The stems do not form cushions but do elongate up to 4 or 5 inches in length. The tube of the corolla is from ½ to ¾ inch long and this is crowned by lobes which extend at right angles. Petal color is variable, but it is usually some shade of pink. Look for this species in sagebrush communities where the soil has good drainage and gravel. Many species of the genus *Phlox* have been brought into cultivation especially for rock-garden use. Flowering occurs in May and early June.

NORTHERN SWEETVETCH
Hedysarum boreale   Pea Family

Since the flowers of this species closely resemble those of milkvetches and locoweeds, it is prudent to look for the fruit to verify identification. Sweetvetch pods are flattened and are remarkably constricted between the seeds so that each section appears round. The other mentioned plants have typical fruits shaped like garden peas. Inhabiting gravelly or sandy soils in stream channels or terraces in both parks, this plant is found from mid to high elevations, usually in grassland vegetation. Leaves are pinnately compound with many leaflets. The keel of the flower is nearly straight and longer than the wings. June and July are the months for flowering.

FIREWEED
Evening Primrose Family
Epilobium angustifolium

The common name of this plant refers to its ability to populate burned-over and logged areas with a beautiful cover of deep pink flowers. The reddish stems, bearing many alternate lance-like leaves, may reach a height of 6 feet. The slightly irregular flowers are built on a plan of four. In the fall the slender inflorescence takes on a fluffy white appearance because the tips of the seeds are covered with long white hairs. The forests in this area are showered annually with the airborne seed of this plant. Successful invasion, however, depends on the reduced plant competition of disturbed sites. Boiling young shoots is one way to use Fireweed for food.

FEW-FLOWERED SHOOTING STAR
Primrose Family
Dodecatheon pulchellum

The Shooting Star species (three in the two parks) are similar to the cultivated Cyclamen, having flowers in an umbel and petals which are reflexed backward. The flowering stems grow to 12 inches tall and flowers are from ½ to 1 inch long. All members of the genus *Dodecatheon* are called Shooting Star because of their hanging flowers with their sepals and petals bent backward 180 degrees. The stamens form a dark-colored cone around the style. The Few-flowered Shooting Star is a very variable species especially in regard to leaf shape and margins. Flowering may begin in early June in the valleys.

LEWIS MONKEYFLOWER   Figwort Family
Mimulus lewisii

Hiking the canyon trails from 7,000 to 9,000 feet, one is very likely to see the Lewis Monkeyflower growing close to some small stream or on a wet ledge. It was named after Lewis of the Lewis and Clark Expedition. Captain Lewis found this plant near Glacier National Park in 1805. The 5 petals are united into a tube with spreading corolla lobes (3 down and 2 up). The lower lobes usually have yellow ridges with hairs. Such a structure is well adapted to specialized pollinators such as bees and hummingbirds. When a bee crawls into the wide opening of the corolla for nectar, its back is dusted with pollen which it carries to the next flower. As the bee crawls into the tube of the second flower, its back brushes pollen onto the spreading lobes of the stigma.

TAPERTIP ONION
Allium acuminatum   Lily Family

Wild onions have been used for their edible bulbs since ancient times, both in the New and Old Worlds. The Indians ate the bulbs raw or cooked them with other food. Many mammals, such as bear and elk, also use these odoriferous plants. There are about 500 species of *Allium* in the world, and all have the same distinctive flowering structure — 3 sepals, 3 petals, 6 stamens and 3 fused carpels. The flowering stem of Tapertip Onion is 6 to 12 inches tall. The petal tips are tapered and spreading. The basal leaves are grasslike and usually wither by flowering time in June or early July. Look for them on moraines and sagebrush flats.

ELEPHANTHEAD   Figwort Family
    Pedicularis groenlandica

ELEPHANTHEAD   Figwort Family
    Pedicularis groenlandica

A close examination of a single flower will reveal why this plant has such a descriptive common name. The upper lip of the corolla has a long up-curving beak which encloses the style. Two petals of the lower lip are shaped like ears. Together the parts of this irregular flower have an amazing resemblance to an elephant's head. The leaves are all pinnately divided and quite fern-like. Look for the purple racemes in wet meadows and along streams from 6,800 to 9,500 feet during July and August. Pollination of individual flowers is brought about by a complex vibrating action of visiting bees.

COMMON INDIAN PAINTBRUSH

Castilleja miniata   Figwort Family

The actual flowers of the eye-catching "Paintbrush" group are narrow, tubular and greenish-yellow. The vivid scarlet of the leafy bracts surrounding the flowers provide the color of this, the most common species, and yet there are several species in the parks whose bracts are whitish, yellow, orange or pink. The calyx generally has 4 lobes, and the corolla has a narrow, folded upper lip and a lower lip which may be 3-lobed or merely toothed. Most Indian Paintbrushes are partial parasites on such plants as sagebrushes and grasses. The root connection established on the hosts provide nutrients and water. For this reason, they usually cannot be cultivated. This species blooms from mid-June to September in woods and meadows.

BROWNS PEONY   Peony Family
Paeonia brownii
This plant is infrequent in both parks; therefore, there should be some excitement in discovering it. Sagebrush areas and open coniferous forests are the habitats to search. Browns Peony is somewhat succulent and has several stems, each bearing several dissected leaves. The single flowers are borne at the tips of curved stems and are up to 3 inches across. There are usually 5 or 6 concave sepals blending with 5 or 6 reddish petals with yellowish margins. The stamens are numerous and fit tightly around 4 or 5 pistils which become follicles. Blooming time is mid-June.

SKYROCKET GILIA; SCARLET GILIA
Phlox Family
Ipomopsis aggregata
This plant adds color to the sagebrush flats during the month of July, but it can also be found in open wooded areas in late August. Usually this species is biennial, producing only a small clump of basal leaves the first year, followed by 1½ to 2½ foot flowering stems the second year. The flaring corolla lobes are bright red with a yellowish mottling on the inside. The flowers are especially attractive to hummingbirds that thrust their bills down the tube of the corolla seeking nectar at the base. In the hovering and collecting process the bird's head becomes covered with pollen, and when it hovers at the next flower, pollination is assured. [Pictured on front cover]

STEER'S-HEAD
Fumitory Family
Dicentra uniflora
One of the most beautiful harbingers-of-spring, the Steer's-head is unique in its flower structure. Like other bleeding-hearts in the family it has 2 sepals, 4 petals and 6 stamens. Only 2 to 4 inches tall, the plant has a single flower at the tip of each leafless stem. The longer outer petals are curved backward, exposing the tops of the inner petals. The whole flower is about ¾ inch long, and it is easy to see the connection to the common name. The long petioled leaves are delicate and subdivided into many oblanceolate segments. Growing in gravelly soil, it is usually found in the sagebrush community and on montane ridges. It flowers within a few days after the snow melts.

FIRECHALICE; WILD FUCHSIA
Evening Primrose Family
Zauschneria garrettii
(Epilobium canum)

The stems of this plant are somewhat woody and tend to become prostrate on the gravelly slopes of the canyons. The scarlet flower-tube (hypanthium) is about 1 inch long and trumpet-shaped. Four sepals and four 2-lobed petals are inserted at its top. A long slender style bearing the 4-lobed stigma protrudes beyond the petals. The flowers with their red color, tubular form and abundant nectar attract hummingbirds especially in late summer. The leaves are usually hairy and have a many toothed margin. Flowering may continue into the late fall in spite of the early frosts.

SKY PILOT
Phlox Family
Polemonium viscosum

Sky Pilot is truly a symbol of the lofty alpine zone. The clusters of funnel or bell-shaped flowers sparkle with various shades of blue to blue-violet. The 5 yellow or orange anthers contrast vividly with the petals, and the bright orange pollen is often seen on the legs of the bees which systematically forage from plant to plant. This and other *Polemonium* species have one striking feature in common — a fetid skunky odor. This fragrance is traceable to the sticky glandular hairs that cover leaves and stems. The leaves are up to 6-7 inches long and pinnately compound; each leaflet is divided into 3-5 lobes. Flowering occurs in July and August. A taller valley dwelling species, *P. occidentale,* grows in wet meadows of the National Elk Refuge north of the town of Jackson.

WESTERN MONKSHOOD   Buttercup Family
Aconitum columbianum
Monkshoods inhabit wet meadows and stream banks up to 9,000 feet in the
major canyons. The stem is stout and varies from 2 to 6 feet. The upper sepal
of this irregular flower is modified into a hood-shaped structure and is responsible for the common name. In addition there are 2 broad sepals at the side and
2 small below. Concealed within the hood are 2 petals and numerous stamens.
The flowers are generally purple, but occasional albinos occur. This species depends upon bumblebees for pollination; smaller insects haven't the strength to
push aside floral parts to reach the nectar. Like the Larkspur, the plants contain
poisonous alkaloids, especially in the roots.

THICKSTEM ASTER   Sunflower Family
Aster integrifolius
While many species of asters are hard to separate, the Thickstem Aster has some distinctive features that set it apart. The rather tall stems (10 to 24 inches) have only
a few flower heads in a narrow inflorescence. The sparse purple rays vary from 10
to 25 and surround the yellow-orange disk flowers. The involucral bracts below the
flowers and flower stalks are covered with glandular hairs. Late August and early September are less drab because of this ragged but beautiful perennial. This particular
aster will inhabit disturbance sites as well as dry meadows and open forests.

LOW LARKSPUR
Buttercup Family
Delphinium nuttallianum

This species is widely distributed
from sagebrush areas to mountain
valleys and even to rocky ridges near
treeline. The plant is commonly less
than 2 feet tall, and the stem devel-
ops from clusters of tuberous roots.
The generic name, *Delphinium,* is
derived from the Latin *delphinius*
meaning "dolphin," a reference to
dolphin-shaped flowers in some
species. The upper sepal in this
genus extends backward into a prominent spur. The spur sepal plus 4
other sepals expand to reveal 4 smaller petals of lighter color. Hummingbirds are frequent visitors to the
flowers. Although it has practically
no effect on park wildlife, the Low
Larkspur contains a combination of
alkaloids which are toxic to livestock.

MOUNTAIN BLUEBELL
Mertensia ciliata

Borage Family

Reaching a height of 3 feet, this showy Mountain Bluebell inhabits subalpine areas particularly along streams. The lanceolate, alternate leaves and tender stems are enjoyed by many animals of the parks. The tubular flowers are purplish in bud but rapidly turn blue as the blossoms expand to full size. The 5 fused petals that form the bell have a lower tube and a flaring limb. Five stamens are attached to the inside of the corolla. Look for this species on the trail to Lake Solitude or while traveling the highway over Dunraven Pass. The peak blooming time is late July and early August.

MOUNTAIN PENSTEMON
Penstemon montanus

Figwort Family

One common name for this group, Beardstongue, refers to the presence of a sterile stamen (tongue) in addition to 4 fertile stamens. No pollen is formed by the sterile stamen, but it is commonly covered with a "beard" or a tuft of hairs. There are over 200 species of *Penstemon* in western North America, but the identification is difficult and requires careful observation of minute flower detail. The flowers are usually borne in groups of 2 or more in the axils of opposite leaves. The Penstemons, in general, are found in open rather dry and rocky habitats. The species shown here is most often seen in the alpine ecosystem, but may be found as low as 8,000 feet in Yellowstone. The anthers are woolly with tangled hairs.

COMMON BLUE-EYED-GRASS   Iris Family
Sisyrinchium idahoense

Whether seen from the board walks of the geysers or along the banks of the Snake River, these miniatures of the Iris Family will always draw favorable comments. The flattened stems are about 6 to 12 inches tall and are topped with 1 to 5 flowers. Where the 3 sepals and 3 petals join there is a yellow center. Note also that each perianth member is tipped with a minute point. The 3 stamens are joined with the style to form a central column. This column plus the inferior ovary are the features that set this plant apart as a member of the Iris Family. The genus *Sisyrinchium* is a perplexing group with many intergrading variants named as species. Flowering occurs in July and August.

FRINGED GENTIAN   Gentian Family
Gentianopsis detonsa
(Gentianella detonsa)

This annual species has numerous leaves in a tuft at the base of the stem and the flowers are borne singly on long stalks. The 4 petals are fused into a corolla about 2 inches long, the lobes of which are delicately fringed. The Park Service chose this plant as the official flower of Yellowstone National Park. In this area it is common and blooms throughout the summer season, beginning in June in the warm earth of the geyser basins. However, in Grand Teton National Park it occurs in rather limited areas. Look for flowers along the main highway between Jackson Lake Dam and the Jackson Lake Lodge.

ROUNDLEAF HAREBELL
Bellflower Family
Campanula rotundifolia

The generic name of this perennial means "little bell," and the specific name, *rotundifolia*, refers to the roundish, heart-shaped, basal leaves. While the basal leaves wither early, the narrow leaves of the stem remain. A conspicuous feature of the flowers is that, although the buds grow erect, the open blossoms droop or are horizontal, protecting the pollen from rain. Occasionally, white flowers will grace the stems of this circumboreal species. Throughout July and August this delicate herb is frequent in open coniferous forests and along roadside cuts. In rock gardens this plant spreads rapidly by rhizomes.

SILVERY LUPINE
Lupinus argenteus   Pea Family

This genus is taxonomically very difficult; as a result, botanists have described about 600 species. The problem with this group arises from the fact that many species hybridize, yielding a broad spectrum of intergrading forms. Lupines as a group are easily recognized by typical pealike flowers, hairy fruit pods, and the palmately compound leaf with 5 to several leaflets at the top of a long petiole. The plants grow in dense colorful clumps in the sagebrush community as well as open pine forests. Lupines benefit the soil because there are nitrogen-fixing bacteria in their root nodules; however, lupines contain lupinine and other related toxic alkaloids which may have serious consequences for livestock.

COMMON SELFHEAL
Prunella vulgaris   Mint Family

Common Selfheal was once esteemed for healing wounds, but now it is considered only good as a refreshing, minty tea. The flowers are pink to purple. The corolla is 2-lipped with the upper lip forming a hood, and the center lobe of the lower lip is delicately fringed. The bilabiate calyx is purplish and covered with long hairs. There are 4 stamens in 2 sets. Like other members of the Mint Family, the stems are square and have opposite leaves. Notice also that the flowers are set in rings around the spike with only a few flowers blooming at any one time. This plant inhabits stream banks, lake shores and moist trailsides. Flowering occurs in July and August.

SILKY PHACELIA
Phacelia sericea   Waterleaf Family

The genus *Phacelia* is large and perplexing with at least 150 species in North America. Silky Phacelia, however, is one of the easiest to recognize. The stems which reach up to 20 inches in height have leaves which are pinnately cleft. The dense elongated flowering spikes may be up to 9 inches long. The 5 petals are fused at the base forming a saucer. The dark purple stamens extend well beyond the corolla, giving the inflorescence a fuzzy appearance. The specific name, *sericea*, means "silky" and refers to the silky pubescence covering stems and leaves. This perennial grows in well drained soils of trails and roadsides from 6,500 to 8,500 feet and flowers in July and August.

BLUE CAMAS
Camassia quamash   Lily Family

This member of the Lily Family is an onion-like plant arising from a bulb which has been used by many Native American tribes as an important food. Wet meadows east of Jackson Lake and meadows adjacent to Yellowstone Lake are the best places to look for this June blooming species. A leafless flowering stalk reaches a height of about 18 inches and is crowned with a loose cluster of purplish-blue flowers, 1 to 1½ inches in diameter. Harrington (see references) says the bulb seems to be lacking in starch, although the sugar content is high. Harrington also reports that many local Indian wars were fought over the collecting rights to certain Blue Camas meadows.

WATERLEAF   Waterleaf Family
Hydrophyllum capitatum
The first visitors of each travel season will find this handsome plant along with Violets and Springbeauties, especially in open wooded areas. The light violet to purple flowers (about ⅜ inch long) are in a dense, ball-like cluster which has a fringed appearance because the anthers and bilobed stigmas are held conspicuously above the tubular corolla. The specific epithet, *capitatum,* means a "head" and refers to the flower cluster. *Hydrophyllum* is Greek meaning "waterleaf," but the meaning in this case is obscure. The stems and leaves are somewhat succulent, and the latter are pinnately cleft and fernlike. The flowering head is sometimes hidden by the leaves that are higher on the stems.

SUGARBOWL; HAIRY CLEMATIS   Buttercup Family
Clematis hirsutissima
This extraordinary herbaceous plant commonly reaches a height of 1 to 2 feet. The flower has no petals and the purple petaloid sepals are somewhat obscured on the outer surface by a covering of cobwebby hairs. Many stamens and pistils are enclosed in the perianth bowl. The fruits of Sugarbowl are achenes with long feathery styles. The leaves are opposite and are 2 to 4 times pinnately dissected. Because of thickness and wrinkled texture of the sepals, the plant has been called Leather Flower. The specific epithet, *hirsutissima*, means "very hairy." The plant grows with big sagebrush or in open pine forests, blooming in late June or early July. Unlike most other *Clematis* species it is not a vine.

ALPINE FORGET-ME-NOT   Borage Family
Eritrichium nanum
Many cushion plants occur in the alpine ecosystem, but the brilliant blue and delicate fragrance makes this cushion plant unforgettable. Grand Teton National Park selected this species as its official plant, suggesting the beauty of the alpine zone. One open flower is considerably smaller than a thumbtack, and when a bumblebee visits the flower, its body covers the entire perianth. Note the yellow center of the corolla which leads to the hidden stamens. Cushion plants in general reach only a few inches above the soil, and as a result avoid the harsh environmental conditions such as continuous wind. The generic name, *Eritrichium*, means "woolly hair" in reference to the woolly pubescence of the leaves.

WILD BLUE FLAX;
LEWIS FLAX
Linum lewisii Flax Family

Wild Blue Flax inhabits dry rocky soils of the valleys and up to subalpine ridges. The numerous flowers are borne on slender stems 1 to 2 feet tall which bend and bow to every passing breeze. The 5 blue petals (most color films do not record this hue correctly) are extremely fragile and will fall off at the slightest handling. The 5 styles are longer than the 5 stamens. The blossoms open early in the morning and usually close late in the afternoon. The brown seed capsules, about ¼ inch across, contain numerous seeds that are rich in oil. Native Americans of the Pacific Northwest used the plant to make their thread and fishing tackle. The plant blooms from June through August

WHIPPLE PENSTEMON
Penstemon whippleanus

Figwort Family

The flowers of this Penstemon come in two color phases — deep wine lavender and the less common creme with purple veins. As with many other Penstemons, it has multiple stems, opposite leaves, and a corolla with 5 joined petals. A hand lens will reveal the numerous glandular hairs that cover the sepals and petals. There are 4 stamens with anthers and a fifth stamen without an anther but usually with a cluster of hairs at its tip. In our parks the plants appear on wooded slopes in the canyons and continue upward into the alpine zone. Approximately 12 species of Penstemons are to be found in both parks.

GIANT HYSSOP; HORSEMINT
Agastache urticifolia   Mint Family

As with other mints, the combination of opposite leaves, square stems and irregular flowers (bilateral symmetry) sets it apart. The plants are often described as coarse because of the clumps of stems up to 3½ feet tall, ragged leaf margins and fuzzy appearing spikes. The 4 stamens are in two sets (2 long and 2 short) and protrude noticeably beyond the corolla tube. As the flower wanes in August many nutlets (4 per flower) are produced in the inflorescences. These are consumed by browsing animals and birds. The generic name comes from the Greek *agan* meaning "much" and *stachys* meaning "ear of grain," referring to the flower spikes. This species forms dense clumps along trails in open woods.

CLUSTERED BROOMRAPE   Broomrape Family
Orobanche fasciculata

A flower enthusiast should experience a thrill upon finding this small (up to 6 inches high) true parasite. It has been reported growing on a variety of host plants, but sagebrush plants seem to be the most frequent host. Usually there is a thick underground stem whose haustoria penetrate the host's roots to withdraw water and nutrition. The calyx and tubular corolla are brownish to yellowish with some purplish color within the tube. There are 2 pair of stamens, and the overall appearance is that of a miniature *Penstemon* species. Parasitism as a way of life is often looked upon with disdain, but it is actually a highly successful strategy that has evolved many times in a number of plant families.

WOODLAND PINEDROPS   Wintergreen Family
Pterospora andromedea
The reddish-brown stem may reach a height of 3½ feet, and it is covered with sticky hairs. The leaves are small and scale-like on the lower half of the stem. Careful research has shown that this plant is a mycrotroph, which means that it lives as a parasite on soil fungi. The fungi in turn have direct connection to the roots of forest trees. Thus the fungus permits Pinedrops to parasitize the trees indirectly. The urn-shaped nodding flowers have a 5-parted calyx and a united corolla. The fruits of the raceme mature into brown capsules that release great quantities of minute winged seeds. Stems grow for only one year, but the dried stems may last for several years. Flowering begins in July and continues into mid August.

STRIPED CORALROOT
Corallorhiza striata   Orchid Family

Coralroot Orchids are devoid of the green pigment, chlorophyll, and cannot manufacture their own food. They are completely dependent on a group of saprophytic fungi in the duff of the coniferous forest. Thus the coralroots live as parasites on the saprophytic fungi, and therefore they can survive in very shady habitats since they do not need light for photosynthesis. The broad lower petal (lip) is almost completely purple, and the upper petals and sepals are brownish overall with 3 red to purple stripes. The leaves are reduced to sheaths on the lower parts of the stem. Even though the generic name means "coral root," there is no root per se but rather a hard mass of rhizome tissue associated with a fungus. The rhizomes may remain dormant for years after producing flowering stems.

SPOTTED CORALROOT   Orchid Family
Corallorhiza maculata

Most members of the Orchid Family, including the coralroots, are becoming increasingly less frequent as man progressively destroys their moist forest habitats. The transplanting of coralroots should not be attempted because the coral-like rhizomes are associated with a complex group of fungi that are found only in natural sites. Slender asparagus-like stems appear in late June and early July and quickly develop racemes with 10 to 25 captivating flowers. The specific epithet, *maculata,* means "spotted," and is given because of the purple to brown spots on the 3-lobed white lip of the flower. A yellow tubular ovary twists and elongates after the perianth shrivels and produces millions of miniscule seeds. Albino or partially albino individuals are occasionally encountered.

LEOPARD LILY;
PURPLESPOT FRITILLARIA
Fritillaria atropurpurea Lily Family

Leopard Lilies are easily missed if the park visitor isn't watching for them. The fast growing stem (up to 20 inches tall) bears 2 to 4 nodding flowers. The stem and narrow leaves are derived from a flattened bulb with many bulblets for asexual reproduction. When one of the flowers is examined closely, the yellowish spots are revealed against a bronze or purple background. There are 6 perianth members and 6 stamens. The odor emanating from the open flower, especially in the morning, is very unpleasant to humans, but very attractive to flies, which are probably responsible for pollination. The plant grows in open forests or grassy slopes; it generally flowers in June.

WESTERN CONEFLOWER   Sunflower Family
Rudbeckia occidentalis

August is the month to watch for this stout perennial which varies between 3 to 6 feet tall. The distinctive flowering heads are on tall leafy stems. The colorful ray flowers seen in other composites are lacking in this species, and yet the numerous disk flowers are obviously displayed on a cylindrical cone nearly 2 inches long. In spite of the diminutive size of the disk flowers, they provide considerable nectar and pollen for frequent visits of bumblebees. The plants can be found in disturbance sites such as trailsides or in shady places near Gibbon Meadows and Tower Falls. In Grand Teton the plant grows along the highway north of Colter Bay.

PARTS OF A FLOWER

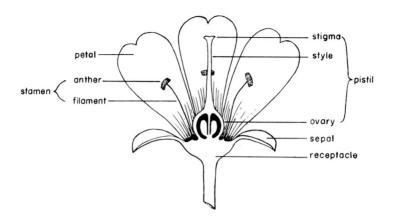

GLOSSARY

Circumboreal — Occurring all the way around the northern latitudes.

Disk flower — A central flower of a composite inflorescence (such as the center of a sunflower).

Ecosystem — A system formed by the interaction of a community of plants and animals with their environments.

Esker — A serpentine ridge of gravelly soil formed by a pocket gopher.

Follicle — A dry fruit formed from a single carpel, splitting open along one edge only.

Involucre — A set of leafy bracts beneath an inflorescence, especially in the Sunflower Family.

Nectar — The sweet secretion of a flower which attracts insects and birds.

Palmate — With three of more lobes, leaflets or veins arising from a common point.

Perennial — Living year after year.

Perianth — The collective term applied to the sepals and petals.

Pinnate — Having two rows of parts or appendages along an axis, like barbs on a feather.

Pollination — Transfer of pollen from the anther to the stigma by such agents as wind, insects and birds.

Pubescence — The various types of hairs that cover the surface of a plant.

Raceme — An elongated inflorescence with a single main axis along which stalked flowers are arranged.

Ray flower — The straped-shaped marginal flowers of the Sunflower Family; each ray flower is complete with a corolla and essential organs.

Rhizome — An underground stem or branch; differing from a root in possessing nodes and internodes.

Umbel — An inflorescence in which flower stalks radiate from a single point like an umbrella.

INDEX

61

CREDITS

Book design by L. Goff Dowding

Front cover design by Richard Firmage

PHOTOS

Franz Camenzind, 5, 17, 24b, 48b, 49t

Bob Cooper, 54t, 56b

Jeff Foott, 45t

Jackie Gilmore, 12b, 28b, 31b

Jeff Hogan, 58b

Leo Larson, 47

Maria Mantas, 10t, 12t, 13, 15t, 24t, 25t, 32b, 34, 36, 38b, 39, 41t, 53t

Jim Olson, 30b, 35b, 37b, 46b, 51t

Danny On, 37t, 52t, back cover b

Pat O'Hara, front cover photograph of balsamroot

Janet J. Rogers, 7b

Richard J. Shaw, 6, 7t, 8, 9, 10b, 11, 14, 15b, 16, 18, 19, 20, 21, 22, 23, 25b, 26, 27, 28t, 29, 30t, 31t, 32t, 33, 35t, 38t, 40, 41b, 42, 43, 44, 45b, 46t, 48t, 49b, 50, 51b, 52b, 53b, 54b, 55, 56t, 57, 58t, 59

SELECTED REFERENCES

Anderson, B. 1976. *Wildflower Name Tales*. Century One Press, Colorado Springs, Colorado.

Dorn, R. D. 1988. *Vascular Plants of Wyoming*. Mountain West Publishing, Cheyenne, Wyoming.

Harrington, H. D. 1967. *Edible Native Plants of the Rocky Mountains*. University of New Mexico, Albuquerque, New Mexico.

Luer, C. A. 1975. *The Native Orchids of the U.S. and Canada*. New York Botanical Garden, New York.

Shaw, R. J. 1981. *Plants of Yellowstone and Grand Teton National Parks*. Wheelwright Press, Salt Lake City, Utah.

Weiner, M. A. 1972. *Earth Medicine — Earth Foods*. Collier Books, New York.

Whitson, T. D. et al. 1987. *Weeds and Poisonous Plants of Wyoming and Utah*. University of Wyoming, Cooperative Extension Service, Laramie, Wyoming.

Zwinger, A. H. and B. E. Willard. 1972. *Land Above the Trees*. Harper and Row, New York.